W9-DDA-822

Jr. Graphic Biographies™

HERNÁN CORTÉS

and the Fall of the Aztec Empire

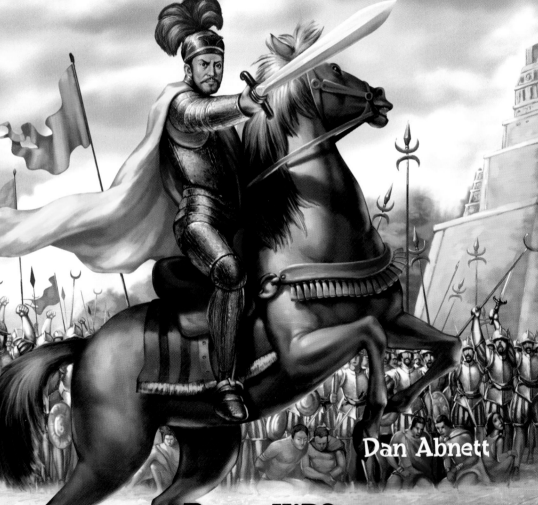

Dan Abnett

PowerKiDS
press™
New York

Published in 2007 by The Rosen Publishing Group, Inc.
29 East 21st Street, New York, NY 10010

First Edition

Editors: Joanne Randolph and Nel Yomtov
Book Design: Julio A. Gil
Illustrations: Q2A

Library of Congress Cataloging-in-Publication Data

Abnett, Dan.
  Hernán Cortés and the fall of the Aztec Empire / Dan Abnett.— 1st ed.
      p. cm. — (Jr. graphic biographies)
  Includes index.
  ISBN (10) 1-4042-3391-1 (13) 978-1-4042-3391-1 (lib. bdg.) —
ISBN (10) 1-4042-2144-1 (13) 978-1-4042-2144-4 (pbk.)
  1. Cortés, Hernán, 1485–1547—Juvenile literature. 2. Mexico—History—Conquest,
1519–1540—Juvenile literature. I. Title. II. Series.
F1230.C385H46 2007
972'.02092—dc22

                                        2006002706

Manufactured in the United States of America

CONTENTS

MAIN CHARACTERS

Hernán Cortés (1485–1547) Spanish **conquistador** who overthrew the Aztec **empire** and won Mexico for the crown of Spain. Cortés is sometimes spelled Cortéz.

Montezuma (1466–1520) Aztec emperor who was taken prisoner by the Spanish conquistadors and forced to carry out their wishes. Montezuma is sometimes spelled Moctezuma.

Pedro de Alvarado (c. 1485–1541) One of the best soldiers among the conquistadors and one of Cortés's most trusted officers. It is believed he was also one of the most unkind to the native people.

HERNÁN CORTÉS AND THE FALL OF THE AZTEC EMPIRE

THE AZTECS LIVED IN WHAT IS NOW CENTRAL AND SOUTHERN MEXICO. THE LAND WAS RICH FOR GROWING CROPS. IT WAS ALSO RICH IN GOLD.

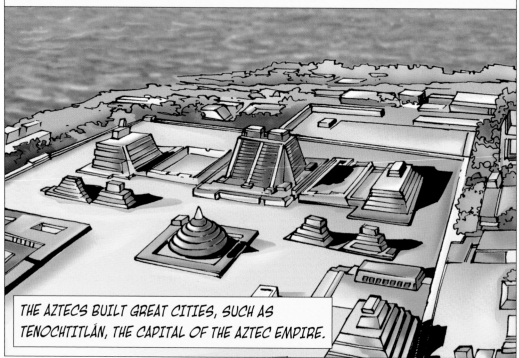

THE AZTECS BUILT GREAT CITIES, SUCH AS TENOCHTITLÁN, THE CAPITAL OF THE AZTEC EMPIRE.

HERNÁN CORTÉS WAS A SPANISH CONQUISTADOR. HE WAS LIVING IN CUBA WHEN HE HEARD TALES OF THE GOLD-FILLED LAND OF THE AZTECS.

HE DECIDED TO LEAD AN **EXPEDITION** TO CLAIM THE AZTECS' GOLD.

NOVEMBER 8, 1519. AFTER NINE MONTHS TRAVELING ACROSS CENTRAL AMERICA, CORTÉS AND HIS CONQUISTADORS REACHED THE CITY OF TENOCHTITLÁN.

THE STORIES SAY THAT THIS PLACE IS FULL OF GOLD AND **TREASURE**. SOON THEY WILL BE MINE!

CORTÉS TRAVELED OVER ONE OF THE **CAUSEWAYS** THAT LED TO THE CITY.

HE MET MONTEZUMA, RULER OF THE AZTECS.

I BRING YOU GREETINGS FROM THE COURT OF SPAIN.

CORTÉS NEEDED TWO **TRANSLATORS** TO SPEAK TO MONTEZUMA.

MONTEZUMA TREATED CORTÉS AND HIS MEN WELL. ONE DAY HE HONORED CORTÉS BY TAKING HIM TO THE TOP OF A GREAT TEMPLE.

WHAT A TRULY GLORIOUS PLACE. IT IS A SHAME IT WILL NO LONGER BE MONTEZUMA'S!

AFTER EIGHT DAYS IN THE CITY, CORTÉS HAD A PLAN. HE TOLD HIS PLAN TO HIS MOST FAITHFUL **DEPUTY**, PEDRO DE ALVARADO.

PEDRO, I KNOW HOW I CAN CONTROL THE CITY!

CORTÉS'S PLAN WAS TO RULE THE AZTEC PEOPLE THROUGH MONTEZUMA. CORTÉS HAD MONTEZUMA ARRESTED.

MONTEZUMA SAYS HE WILL LEAD HIS PEOPLE AS YOU WISH.

MONTEZUMA SAYS THAT HE FEARS HIS PEOPLE WILL RISE AGAINST US.

MONTEZUMA WAS NOT THE ONLY WORRIED ONE.

I DARE NOT SLEEP, IN CASE THEY ATTACK. I WEAR MY **ARMOR** TO BED.

HOW LONG WILL YOU BE ABLE TO CONTROL THE AZTECS WITHOUT USING FORCE?

DO NOT WORRY. I CONTROL MONTEZUMA.

CORTÉS MADE MONTEZUMA SHOW HIM WHERE THE AZTEC TREASURE WAS HIDDEN.

HA! THE KING WISHES FOR US TO TAKE THE TREASURE AND LEAVE!

CORTÉS WAS TOLD THAT THE GOVERNOR OF CUBA HAD SENT PORFILO DE NARVÁEZ TO ARREST HIM. CORTÉS HAD DISOBEYED ORDERS.

HE WILL NOT STOP ME! I WILL TAKE POWER!

IN MAY 1520, CORTÉS MARCHED MOST OF HIS MEN OUT OF TENOCHTITLÁN.

FIRST I MUST TAKE CARE OF NARVÁEZ. THEN I WILL RETURN AND **DEFEAT** THE AZTECS.

CORTÉS LEFT PEDRO DE ALVARADO IN CHARGE OF THE CITY. ALVARADO HAD A FORCE OF ABOUT 100 MEN.

IF THE AZTECS WANTED TO FIGHT US, THEY WOULD WIN. WE MUST HAVE A PLAN TO BEAT THEM.

THE AZTECS ASK TO HOLD THEIR YEARLY **FESTIVAL** IN THE CITY SQUARE.

VERY WELL. THEY HAVE MY PERMISSION.

WE WILL ATTACK DURING THE FESTIVAL.

WE WILL SHOW THEM HOW STRONG WE ARE!

THE SMALL SPANISH FORCE ATTACKED THE UNARMED AZTECS AND KILLED HUNDREDS.

THE AZTECS FOUGHT BACK.

ALVARADO SENT WORD TO CORTÉS THAT HE WAS IN TROUBLE.

CORTÉS BEAT NARVÁEZ QUICKLY. HE THEN PROMISED GOLD TO ANY OF NARVÁEZ'S MEN WHO WOULD FIGHT THE AZTECS WITH HIM.

CORTÉS RETURNED TO TENOCHTITLÁN. THE AZTECS ATTACKED.

THE SPANIARDS HAD BETTER **WEAPONS** THAN THE AZTECS HAD, BUT THE AZTECS HAD 10 TIMES THE NUMBER OF MEN CORTÉS HAD.

CORTÉS AND HIS MEN SHUT THEMSELVES IN THEIR HEADQUARTERS.

THE AZTECS GATHERED OUTSIDE. THEY WERE **EAGER** TO FIGHT THE CONQUISTADORS.

THE AZTECS AND THE SPANIARDS FOUGHT ON THE CAUSEWAYS.

WHEN ONE AZTEC **WARRIOR** FELL, 10 MORE WERE READY TO TAKE HIS PLACE.

CORTÉS NEEDED A PLAN TO KEEP CONTROL OF THE CITY.

WE WILL USE MONTEZUMA TO END THIS BATTLE.

CORTÉS FORCED MONTEZUMA TO SPEAK TO HIS PEOPLE.

MY PEOPLE, WE MUST STOP THIS FIGHTING. THE SPANIARDS ARE OUR FRIENDS.

THE AZTECS THREW STONES AT MONTEZUMA.

MONTEZUMA DIED A FEW DAYS LATER. THE AZTECS CHOSE A NEW LEADER.

ON JULY 1, 1520, CORTÉS TRIED TO LEAVE TENOCHTITLÁN. THE AZTECS HAD REMOVED THE BRIDGES ON THE CAUSEWAYS.

THE SPANIARDS TRIED TO BUILD A BRIDGE USING WHATEVER WOOD THEY COULD FIND.

AN AZTEC GUARD SOUNDED THE ALARM. SOON THE WARRIORS WERE ATTACKING THE SPANISH FORCES.

THE SPANISH COULD NOT ESCAPE.

THE AZTECS CONTINUED TO ATTACK. MANY SPANISH SOLDIERS FELL OVER THE EDGE OF THE CAUSEWAY.

THE AZTECS ALSO FOUGHT THE NATIVES WHO HAD JOINED CORTÉS.

THEY BATTLED ALL NIGHT. MANY SPANIARDS DROWNED, BECAUSE THEY WERE WEIGHTED DOWN WITH GOLD.

FINALLY THE REMAINING SPANIARDS REACHED THE SHORE OF THE LAKE.

CORTÉS'S MEN HAD LOST A BATTLE FOR THE FIRST TIME.

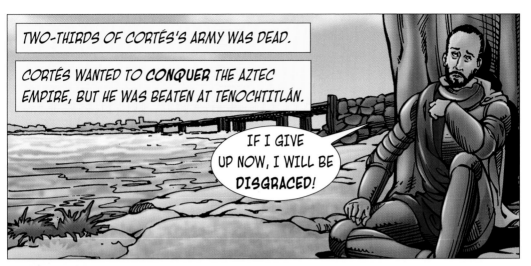

TWO-THIRDS OF CORTÉS'S ARMY WAS DEAD.

CORTÉS WANTED TO **CONQUER** THE AZTEC EMPIRE, BUT HE WAS BEATEN AT TENOCHTITLÁN.

IF I GIVE UP NOW, I WILL BE **DISGRACED!**

THIS IS *LA NOCHE TRISTE.**

* THIS MEANS "THE SAD NIGHT."

CORTÉS TOOK HIS MEN NORTH. THEY NEEDED TO REST AND GET READY FOR THEIR NEXT BATTLE.

THE AZTECS ATTACKED CORTÉS'S FORCES WHENEVER THEY COULD.

A WEEK LATER THE SPANIARDS MET A HUGE ARMY ON THE PLAIN OF OTUMBA.

THAT IS THEIR LEADER! IF WE TAKE HIM, THEY WILL RUN AWAY.

ADVANCE!

CORTÉS'S PLAN WORKED. HE CAPTURED THE NATIVE GENERAL, AND THE WARRIORS RAN OFF.

THE AZTECS OF THE TLAXCALA **REGION** WILL FOLLOW YOU. THEY ARE UNHAPPY WITH THEIR OWN LEADERS.

CORTÉS STRENGTHENED HIS ARMY. HE ALSO HAD SUPPLIES BROUGHT IN FROM A NEARBY SPANISH TOWN.

CORTÉS BUILT 13 SHIPS AT TLAXCALA SO HE COULD CONTROL THE LAKE AT TENOCHTITLÁN. THEY WOULD BE TAKEN APART FOR THE MARCH AND THEN REBUILT.

CORTÉS TALKED MANY OF THE AZTECS INTO JOINING HIM.

IF THEY DO NOT JOIN ME, I WILL MAKE THEM MY SLAVES.

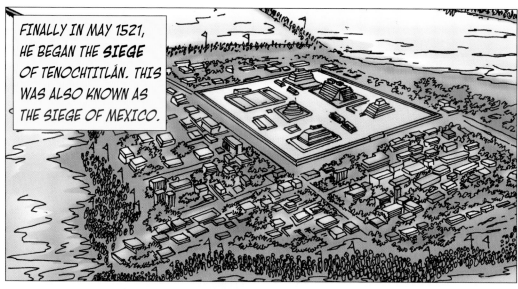

FINALLY IN MAY 1521, HE BEGAN THE **SIEGE** OF TENOCHTITLÁN. THIS WAS ALSO KNOWN AS THE SIEGE OF MEXICO.

THE SPANIARDS DESTROYED THE SYSTEM THAT BROUGHT FRESHWATER TO THE CITY.

THEY WOULD NOT ALLOW IN ANY FOOD.

THE AZTECS FOUGHT ON, EVEN THOUGH THEY HAD NO FOOD OR WATER.

CORTÉS AND HIS ARMY ATTACKED AND WITHDREW SEVERAL TIMES BEFORE THEY FINALLY ENTERED THE CITY.

THE AZTECS WOULD NOT GIVE UP.

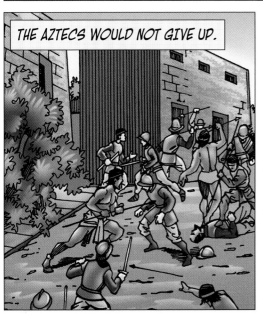

I AM GROWING TIRED OF THEM. NOW WE WILL DRIVE THEM OUT FOR GOOD!

WHEN CORTÉS COULD NOT DEFEAT THE AZTECS, HE SET FIRE TO PARTS OF THEIR CITY.

THE AZTECS WERE DRIVEN OUT OF THEIR HOMES AND TEMPLES.

THE AZTECS FOUGHT THE CONQUISTADORS ON THE ROOFTOPS AND IN THE STREETS.

CORTÉS WAS NOT THE AZTECS' ONLY ENEMY. THEY WERE ALSO DYING FROM SMALLPOX. THIS WAS A SICKNESS BROUGHT TO THEIR LAND BY THE SPANISH.

THE REMAINING AZTECS MADE THEIR LAST STAND IN THE MARKET SQUARE.

THE SPANISH CAPTURED THE NEW AZTEC LEADER, CUAUHTEMOC.

CORTÉS WAS DELIGHTED.

NOW THE CITY WILL BE MINE!

ON AUGUST 13, 1521, THE MARKET SQUARE FELL TO THE SPANIARDS.

CORTÉS HAD WON THE WAR. THE KING OF SPAIN GAVE RICHES AND LAND TO CORTÉS.

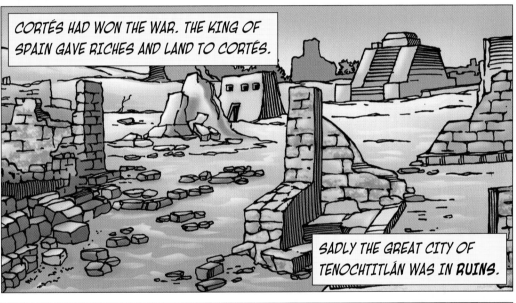

SADLY THE GREAT CITY OF TENOCHTITLÁN WAS IN **RUINS**.

CORTÉS BUILT MEXICO CITY ON THE **SITE** OF TENOCHTITLÁN.

THE NATION OF MEXICO WAS BORN, BUT THE GLORIOUS AZTEC **CIVILIZATION** HAD BEEN DESTROYED.

THE END

TIMELINE

1485 Hernán Cortés is born in Medellín, Spain.

1504 Cortés becomes a soldier and travels to the West Indies for the first time.

1509 Cortés settles in Cuba, a Spanish colony.

1519 In February, Cortés sets sail for Central America.

On November 8, Cortés enters the city of Tenochtitlán by crossing one of its three causeways.

1520 On July 1, Cortés escapes from Tenochtitlán to Tacuba. The evening is known as the Night of Sorrow, or the Sad Night.

1521 In May, Cortés attacks Tenochtitlán with his larger army and many ships.

1522 On August 13, the Siege of Tenochtitlán ends. Cortés takes control of Tenochtitlán.

Cortés is made governor of New Spain, with Tenochtitlán as the capital.

1525 Cortés leads an expedition to Honduras.

1528 Cortés visits Spain for two years.

1540 Cortés returns to Spain one last time.

1547 Cortés dies at his home in Seville, Spain.

GLOSSARY

armor (AR-mer) A type of uniform used in battle to help keep the body safe.

causeways (KAHZ-wayz) Raised roads built across water.

civilization (sih-vih-lih-ZAY-shun) People living in an ordered way.

conquer (KON-ker) To overcome something.

conquistador (kon-KEES-tuh-dor) Spanish soldier who traveled through and conquered large areas of the Americas between 1500 and 1600.

defeat (dih-FEET) To win against someone in a game or battle.

deputy (DEP-yoo-tee) A second in command or an assistant who has the power to act and to make people follow the law.

disgraced (dih-SKRAYSD) To have done something other people disapprove of.

eager (EE-gur) Very interested in doing something.

empire (EM-pyr) A large area controlled by one ruler.

expedition (ek-spuh-DIH-shun) A trip for a special purpose.

festival (FES-tih-vul) A party or special time of feasting.

region (REE-jen) One of the many different parts of Earth.

ruins (ROO-enz) Old, falling-down buildings.

siege (SEEJ) The surrounding of a place, such as a castle or city, to cut off supplies.

site (SYT) The place where a certain event happens.

translators (tranz-LAY-terz) People who help people who speak different languages understand each other.

treasure (TREH-zher) Things of great worth or value.

warrior (WAR-ee-yur) A person who fights in a war.

weapons (WEH-punz) Objects or tools used to wound, disable, or kill.

INDEX

WEB SITES
Due to the changing nature of Internet links, the Rosen Publishing Group, Inc., has developed an online list of Web sites related to the subject of this book. This site is updated regularly. Please use this link to access the list:
www.powerkidslinks.com/jgb/cortes/